The Boston Tea Party

The Boston Tea Party

Steven Kroll

illustrated by Peter Fiore

Holiday House / New York

The Seven Years War was fought in Europe, North America, and India from 1756 to 1763. When it ended, England and Prussia, the largest German state, had defeated France and Austria in Europe. In North America, where the battles became known as the French and Indian War, England forced France to leave Canada.

The war cost England a lot of money. The government was heavily in debt. To pay off that debt, the English Parliament passed laws that raised taxes throughout the country.

Parliament also felt that England should still keep an army in the American colonies. To make Americans help pay that expense, the members passed the Sugar Act in 1764.

The colonists would have to pay new or higher taxes on everything from sugar and coffee to indigo and whale fins shipped from foreign countries, including England. They were furious. They had been paying taxes on goods from countries that might compete with British-American trade, but this was the first time Parliament had taxed them just to raise money for the British government. Besides, the colonists had no representatives in Parliament and no say in the laws that were passed. They felt Parliament had no right to tax them at all.

In protest, many colonists refused to buy English goods. Nevertheless, Parliament passed more tax laws. One of the most unpopular was the Stamp Act of 1765. The colonists would have to buy official stamps or seals to put on their newspapers, pamphlets, and other documents. Sold by agents of the government, the stamps were just like another tax. It was the first time Parliament had taxed American-made items.

Groups of colonists began to meet secretly. They called themselves the Sons of Liberty and tried to get the stamp agents to quit their jobs. More people stopped buying English goods.

The Stamp Act was withdrawn in March 1766, but in June 1767, the Townshend Acts placed taxes on lead, glass, paper, paint, and tea entering America. Now people all over the colonies stopped buying English goods.

Meanwhile, English troops had arrived in Boston in October 1768 to protect the tax officials. On March 5, 1770, a scuffle with the soldiers broke out on King Street. Colonists hurled insults, calling the soldiers "lobsters" and "bloody backs" because of their red uniforms. The soldiers fired their guns, killing four men and a boy. The incident became known as the Boston Massacre.

With so many colonists refusing to buy English goods, English merchants were losing money. Finally, in April 1770, Parliament withdrew the Townshend Acts—except for a small tax on tea of three pence per pound.

The tax on tea made people angry, but with all the other taxes gone, many decided to buy English products again. Still, a large number continued their protest by buying cheaper tea smuggled in from Holland.

As a result, the powerful British East India Company had tons of unsold tea sitting in warehouses in England. If it was not sold soon, the company would go bankrupt. In May 1773, Parliament reacted by lifting the tax that the British East India Company would have to pay on tea shipped to the colonies from England. This meant the price of the tea would be lower when it reached American shores. England hoped that with the lower price, the colonists would start buying British tea again.

But only a few special colonial agents hired by the British East India Company would be allowed to sell the imported tea. Also, the tax on tea entering America remained.

By August, tea agents had been chosen for Boston, Philadelphia, New York, and Charleston, South Carolina. By early October, seven tea ships were on their way to America.

Parliament's decision shocked the colonists. The tax on tea was bad enough, but what if the members decided that only a few agents could sell *other* goods from England as well? Colonial merchants who weren't chosen might be ruined. Local leaders in New York and Philadelphia held mass meetings to get the tea agents to resign and the tea returned to England. Now Boston had to respond.

Sam Adams, John Hancock, and Paul Revere were among the patriots who met by night in the long room above Benjamin Edes's print shop. Edes was the co-publisher of the *Boston Gazette*, the most outspoken newspaper in town. The group was called the Long Room Club.

Together the patriots decided that the tea should be sent back to England, and the agents should go with it to explain why. On Monday, October 18, the *Gazette* published the details of the British East India Company's plan, a plan "destructive to the happiness of every well-wisher to his country." The paper repeated the Long Room Club's demands.

For two weeks, everyone wondered what would happen next. On November 2, a group that included Sam Adams met at the Green Dragon Tavern. They drew up resolutions and sent them to the tea agents by messenger.

Around one in the morning, Boston tea agent Richard Clarke was the first to receive the notice. Two men thrust it in his face. The paper told him to report to the Liberty Tree in Hanover Square at noon that day to resign. Before dawn, the four other tea agents received the same notice.

Later that morning, colonists passed out handbills announcing that not only would the tea agents resign, they would ship the tea back to London. By noon, around five hundred people had gathered at the old elm in Hanover Square.

The tea agents didn't show up. A search party found them hiding at the Clarke warehouse on Long Wharf.

Two town meetings were held at Faneuil Hall, again in hopes the agents would resign. Still, they refused. On November 18, the agents asked the royal governor of Massachusetts, Thomas Hutchinson, to take charge of the tea. Eleven days later, his advisors refused to allow it.

Meanwhile, at the governor's suggestion, several of the agents moved for greater safety to a fort called Castle William—on an island two miles south of Boston Harbor.

On Sunday, November 28, the *Dartmouth*, the first of the English tea ships, anchored off Long Wharf. If the ship's owner did not pay the tax that was due within twenty days, customs officers would seize the tea.

Sam Adams and his "committee of correspondence" organized a mass meeting to take place at Faneuil Hall the morning of November 29. More than five thousand people showed up. The crowd was so large that the meeting had to be moved to the Old South Meeting House. There everyone agreed that the tea should be returned to England and no tax should be paid.

In the afternoon, Francis Rotch, the twenty-three-year-old son of the *Dartmouth*'s owner, appeared at the church with James Hall, the ship's captain. Rotch was told not to unload the tea. Hall was ordered to bring the *Dartmouth* to Rowe's Wharf, where a guard of twenty-five Americans would make sure the tea remained on board. The next day the colonists ordered the ship moved to Griffin's Wharf.

By December 2, the agents in Philadelphia, New York, and Charleston had resigned. Nevertheless, on that day, the ship *Eleanor* reached Griffin's Wharf with more tea. On the 7th, the brig *Beaver* arrived as well.

Governor Hutchinson, safe on his estate in Milton, ordered the British warships *Active* and *Kingfisher* to block Boston Harbor. The troops at Castle William were placed on alert. No ship was to leave Boston without paying the tax that was due.

On December 13, Sam Adams's "committee of correspondence" met with representatives from the five neighboring towns. The committee knew the tax on the tea had to be paid by midnight on December 16. They convinced the meeting that if the tea was not on its way back to England before then, a group of colonists would destroy it.

At a mass meeting the next morning, the colonists told Francis Rotch to apply for documents that would allow the *Dartmouth* to return to England. Because a ship had to be unloaded before it could leave port legally, he was refused. On the morning of the 16th, he was told to apply to Governor Hutchinson for an exit permit. He rode the seven miles to Milton in the rain, but a permit could be granted only if a ship had been cleared by the port. Of course the governor said no.

Meanwhile, there were men preparing for an unusual kind of "tea party" at Griffin's Wharf. Some were well off, but most were apprentices, carpenters, blacksmiths, and farmers. Secretly, in rooms around town, they put on tattered clothes and Indian blankets and smeared their faces with lampblack and grease, soot and red ochre. If they looked like American Indians, it would be hard for anyone to tell who they really were.

By the time Francis Rotch got back to the Old South Meeting House, it was five forty-five and dark. When he said he couldn't get the permit, Sam Adams climbed to the pulpit and declared, "This meeting can do nothing more to save the country!"

Men dressed as Indians were already at the meeting house. War whoops rang out, along with shouts.

"Boston Harbor a tea pot tonight!"

"The Mohawks are come!"

The "Indians" burst through the front door, howling. Many in the crowd followed down Milk Street into Hutchinson and southeastward past Fort Hill to Griffin's Wharf. Along the way, more Indians appeared. They all stopped howling and started marching.

Near the wharf, younger men and boys appeared. Without disguises, they knew the risk they were taking as they joined the groups boarding the three ships.

The tea chests were hoisted on deck, smashed open, and heaved over the side. Smashing the 342 chests was easy, but the tea was wrapped in canvas that blunted the strokes of the hatchets. Also, it was low tide in Boston Harbor. The tea piled up like stacks of hay in water two feet deep.

Everyone worked quickly and quietly. Apart from the tea, nothing was damaged except one padlock that was replaced the next day. But when the tide turned later that night, a fringe of tea could be found all along the edge of the harbor.

By nine o'clock that evening, the job was done. Forming ranks on the wharf, the men disguised as Indians took off their shoes, shook out any remaining bits of tea, and marched into the night.

Afterword

In the spring of 1774, an angry Parliament, supported by King George III, passed the Coercive Acts, also known as the Intolerable Acts.

Boston Harbor would be closed to shipping until the people had paid back the British East India Company for the loss of the tea. The governor or the king would take over the appointment of many colonial officials. Town meetings could not be held without permission of the governor. If necessary, people would have to allow British troops to stay in their own houses as well as in taverns and empty buildings.

The British Parliament hoped these laws would stun the colonies into remaining divided and force Boston to submit to the king. Instead they had the opposite effect. Boston became more defiant. The different colonies united as never before and by summer were sending food, clothing, and other supplies overland to Boston. In September, men from all of the thirteen colonies except Georgia met at the first Continental Congress in Philadelphia to come up with ways of opposing the Coercive Acts. The following April, the war for American independence began.

Important Dates

April 5, 1764	Parliament passes the Sugar Act, the first time the colonies have been taxed to raise money for the British government.
March 22, 1765	Parliament passes the Stamp Act, the first time a direct tax has been placed on America.
March 18, 1766	The Stamp Act is withdrawn.
June 29, 1767	The Townshend Acts place import taxes on lead, glass, paper, paint, and tea.
March 5, 1770	The Boston Massacre occurs. British soldiers kill five colonists.
April 12, 1770	Parliament withdraws the Townshend Acts, except for the tax on tea.
May 10, 1773	The Tea Act allows the British East India Company to sell tea in America without paying an export tax. The import tax of three pence per pound remains.
October 18	The *Boston Gazette* attacks the British East India Company plan.
November 3	The Boston tea agents are asked to resign at noon beneath the Liberty Tree in Hanover Square. They don't show up.
November 28	The tea ship *Dartmouth* arrives in Boston Harbor. The import tax must be paid within twenty days, or the tea will be seized by customs officers.
November 29	A mass meeting is held at the Old South Meeting House.
December 2	The ship *Eleanor* arrives with more tea.
December 7	The brig *Beaver* arrives, also carrying tea.
December 13	Sam Adams and his "committee of correspondence" make plans to destroy the tea if it is not on its way back to England by the evening of December 16.
December 14	A huge mass meeting is held at the Old South Meeting House.
December 16	The Boston Tea Party takes place.
April 19, 1775	The Battle of Lexington and Concord begins the American Revolution.

Copyright © 1998 by Steven Kroll
Illustrations copyright © 1998 by Peter Fiore
ALL RIGHTS RESERVED
Printed in the United States of America

Library of Congress Cataloging-in-Publication Data
Kroll, Steven.
The Boston Tea Party / by Steven Kroll; illustrated by Peter
Fiore. — 1st ed.
p.   cm.
Summary: Describes the events preceding, during, and following the
event which helped precipitate the American Revolutionary War.
ISBN 0-8234-1316-0 (reinforced)
1. Boston Tea Party, 1773—Juvenile literature.   [1. Boston Tea
Party, 1773.   2. United States—History—Revolution, 1775–1783—
Causes.]   I. Fiore, Peter M., ill.   II. Title.
E215.7.K76   1998   96-54855   CIP   AC
973.3'115—dc21
ISBN 0-8234-1557-0 (pbk.)